Love God
Love People
Love Like Jesus

by

Bren Claborn

Dedication

We have been fans of Bren Claborn and her writing for some time now. Her stories, first shared on social media, seem to capture life with a transparency and a practicality and a spiritual depth rarely found together in one place. They have had an impact on us to the point where we wanted to surprise her with a collection of them. We know her personally and enjoy her friendship. She is kind, authentic, funny, and wise. Her husband Gary and son Rocket display similar characteristics as you will see throughout the book. To us, her family truly does "Love God, Love People, and Love Like Jesus." We are proud to call them friends.

Rick and Judi Manis

Forward

I'm 51 years old. My husband and I have been married for almost thirty years. We have three grown daughters and seven grandchildren. Eleven years ago, God blessed us with our bonus baby, a son. As wonderful as all that sounds (and it is), it didn't start out like that. When I was growing up, no one ever told me that I was smart or even that I had potential. It seemed nobody really expected me to succeed at anything, let alone accomplish anything worthwhile. My father was present in our home but absent in my life. I didn't really have any friends and I spent most of my time alone. As I got older, I went from one destructive relationship to the next. It could've all ended there...but that's not my story.

People's opinions and circumstance couldn't hold me because God had a plan and a purpose. And He didn't see me the way others did. God took the most unlikely someone and accomplished extraordinary things...just because He loves me, and He could.

I pray as you read this book that is made up of my thoughts and scribbling that you will be blessed. Once more I'm reminded that God will go far beyond all that I can dream or imagine. And I can dream and imagine a lot! When I feel that what I'm doing is insignificant and unimportant, I ask God to help me remember that everything I do is significant and important in His eyes, because He loves me and He put me here, and no one else can do exactly what I'm doing in exactly the way that I do it (i.e. this little book).

A diamond doesn't start out polished and shining. It once appeared to be nothing special, but with enough pressure and time, it becomes spectacular. I am that diamond.

~ Bren

Table of Contents

Geronimo!

Imagine with me if you will, that you and I and several others are on board an airborne plane when all of a sudden the engine bursts into flames. The pilot rushes out of the cockpit, "We're going to crash!" he yells. He begins to pass out parachutes, giving us a few pointers in the process. We stand in line as he throws open the door. The first passenger steps up and shouts over the wind, "Could I make one request?" "Sure, what is it?" "Is there anyway I could get a pink parachute?" The pilot shakes his head in disbelief, "Isn't it enough that I gave you a parachute at all?" The next one steps up and ask the Captain if he can take away his fear of heights. "No," he replies, "but I'll give you a parachute." Another pleads for a different strategy, "Couldn't we just go down with the plane? We might survive." The pilot smiles and says, "You don't know what you're asking," and gently shoves the fellow out the door. One passenger wants goggles, another wants boots, another wants to wait until the plane is closer to the ground. "You people don't understand," the pilot shouts as he helps us, one by one. "I've given you a parachute; and that's enough."

Only one item is necessary for the jump, and he provides it. He places the tool in our hands. The gift is adequate. But are we content? No. We are restless, anxious, even demanding. I know this story is crazy, and it probably would never happen on a crashing plane, but it happens all the time on earth with people and grace. We, too, ask God to remove fear or change plans, which He usually answers with a gentle shove that leaves us airborne and suspended by His grace. We pray and pray, but what if God says no? What if He calls a young mother home, despite our prayers? Is God still a good God when he says no? Let's back away for a minute and tally this up. God has every right to say no to us. We have every reason to say thanks to Him. The parachute is strong, and the landing will be safe. His grace is sufficient.

A Masterpiece

I love to watch my son when he's passionate about something. He gives it all he's got, holding nothing back! It's who he is. I've watched him work tirelessly this week on a poster for school. All the kids are doing them, so his will be just one of many. But this one is different to him...it's his handiwork, his masterpiece. He's left a little bit of himself on that paper, and I know he'll be proud to put his signature on his work of art.

The same is true with us. In the scheme of nature, Homo Sapiens are not unique. We aren't the only creatures with flesh and hair and blood and hearts. What makes us special is not our body but the signature of God on our lives. We are His works of art. We are created in His image. We are significant, not because of what we do, but because of Whose we are.

I Am For You

I had to make an unpopular decision today. My heart broke as I watched my son's eyes well up with tears, even though I knew it was the best thing for him. I knew he didn't understand today like he will one day when he's older. As a mother, I'd have to say, without a doubt, it sucked!

I can't help but wonder how many times a second God feels this way. Always doing what's best for us, even though we just can't see it at the time. I look back in my own life at all the things that I just couldn't understand at the time, only to take another look and realize that I would have prayed for that exact same answer if I'd known then what I know now.

And while I see the 'big' picture with my son, God sees the 'whole' picture with us. And even though my son may be upset with me right now, I know he doesn't have any doubt that I am for him, not against him. So be encouraged today. God loves you, and He will always do what's best for you. These are the times when we learn to trust Him. After all, God is always for you, not against you.

Guaranteed

One day on a whim I bought a red foil balloon at Walmart. The message "I love you" streamed across the front in billowy script. As I was loading bags into my car, the balloon string slid through my fingers. I stood there watching it float away, and soon it was nothing more than a tiny red dot...finally, just a memory.

Losing that balloon made me think of the way love sometimes vanishes from our lives. Children rebel and distance themselves; spouses or loved ones desert; close friends stop calling. I'm so thankful that God's love is steady; it can sustain us when love here on earth drifts away. In fact it's so reliable that Jesus invites us to abide in His love (John 15:9). He wants us to know it's okay to settle in and get comfortable in His love. We can always remain in God's tender embrace because *"neither death nor life, nor angels nor principalities nor powers, nor things present nor things to come"* (Romans 8:38), or anything else, can ever separate us from His love through Christ. Once we trust Christ as Savior, the guarantee of God's love is ours forever.

Maybe you have watched as love disappeared from your life. You can rest in God's affection. His constant care will keep your heart safely secure.

God IS For You!

God is for you. Not "may be," not "has been," not "was," not "would be," but God is! He is for you. Today. At this hour. At this minute. As you read this sentence. No need to wait in line or come back tomorrow. He is with you. His love won't increase if you are better nor lessen if you are worse. He is for you. Turn to the sidelines: that's God cheering your run. Look past the finish line: that's God applauding your steps. Listen for Him in the bleachers, shouting your name. Too tired to continue? He'll carry you. Too discouraged to fight? He's picking you up. God is for you. If God had a calendar, your birthday would be circled. If He drove a car, your name would be on His bumper. We know He has your name tattooed on His hand (Isaiah 49:16). *"Can a mother forget the baby at her breast and have no compassion on the child she has borne?"* God asks in Isaiah 49:15. What a bizarre question! Can you imagine a mother feeding her infant and then later asking, "What was that baby's name?" No way! But *"though she may forget, I will not forget you,"* God pledges (Isaiah 49:15, NIV).

Like Father, Like Son

Rocket went to work with his dad today. Then they met me at the doctor's office for my appointment at noon. There they stood, side by side, filthy from head to toe. I couldn't help but notice how much like his dad, my son has become. They stand alike, walk alike, they even talk alike. And the thing is, that because Rocket is adopted, it's not by genetics, it's by choice. He wants to be like his daddy. I think back to the time when Gary and I weren't living for the Lord. I consider how much he has changed from the time that he gave his heart to God, till now. Because that too, was a choice that he made...the choice to be like his heavenly Daddy.

An old song runs through my mind, "I want to be like you Lord (because he wants to be like me)." I had to stop and thank God right then and there. I had to thank Him for the godly man that my son calls "Dad." A man that will lead my little boy straight to Jesus... "Oh, be careful little feet where you go, 'cause it's the little feet behind you that are sure to follow..."

A Spoonful of Truth

Where is Mary Poppins when you need her? I know this sounds like I'm longing for the good old days when cheerfully unrealistic movies featured characters like this fictional nanny, but what I'm really longing for are people with a vision for the future that is realistically optimistic. I yearn for joyful, creative people that always look for, and find, the positive in what others think to be negative. People that remind us that, "just a spoonful of sugar makes the medicine go down."

David wrote a song that expressed similar truth. In his words, "*the judgments of the Lord*" are "*sweeter also than honey*" (Palms 19:9-10). Seldom do we hear that truth is sweet. More often than not we hear it is bitter or hard to swallow. But truth is so much more than medicine to treat what's wrong. It's the diet that will prevent disease. It's not an immunization or an injection. It's a gourmet meal that should be presented as a culinary delight, enticing the hungry to "*taste and see that the Lord is good*" (Psalms 34:8).

We sing "Jesus is the sweetest name I know," but some of us present Him as if He's gone sour. Truth is never 'becoming' truth, it simply is. Pure truth, untainted by pride, is the sweetest, most refreshing taste of all to those who hunger for spiritual sustenance...and we have the privilege of serving it to a starving world.

Removing the Clutter

Last night Rocket told me that he had decided to "clean his room." I didn't think much about it, because he likes his room clean and organized. But after awhile I began to wonder what was taking him so long. So I went to check it out. I found my son going through toy tubs, cleaning off shelves, and making a large pile in the middle of the floor. "I'm going through my stuff, and I'm getting rid of some of it that I don't need anymore," he explained. "I just need to remove some of the clutter." Now this really caught me by surprise because ever since he was a baby, he's always been determined to keep everything. (He even has a special place for broken stuff that he just couldn't part with!) So I had to ask, "Why now? What's changed?" With a shrug of his shoulders, he said, "I don't know...I guess I did."

I find it is sometimes the same way in both our physical and spiritual lives. Sometimes, as we grow and change, we just need to let go of some old junk and reduce some of the clutter. More often than not, we find the liberty we all so desperately want, in learning to let go. And as we learn to turn loose of the things that leave us stressed and unorganized, just as my son discovered, we find a peace and a satisfaction that will leave us asking, "Oh man, why didn't I do this sooner?"

My Child

While we were in the park this afternoon, I watched as a woman approached my son, leaned over, and got right in his face. Even from a distance, I could tell she was chewing him out. I could see the look of fear and devastation in his eyes. (Clearly she didn't realize that his momma was only about twenty feet away.) Long story short, my conversation with this woman ended with me saying, "Don't you ever talk to my son like that again! If you have a problem with him, you take it up with me. Even if he had done something wrong, it'll be me, not you, who deals with him, because he's 'my' child!"

Now I'm here to tell you that the enemy wasted no time telling me how 'bad' I had handled the situation. "Well, you really blew that! What happened to 'Love like Jesus'?" After a few minutes of that, I'm sure I had that same look of devastation on my own face. But then I heard it...the voice of the Father...and this is what I heard Him say to my accuser, "Don't you ever talk to My daughter like that again! If you have a problem with her, you take it up with Me. Even if she had done something wrong, it'll be Me, not you, who deals with her because she is 'My' child!"

Losing the Game

He gathered his equipment, put his bag on his shoulder, headed out of the dugout and toward the car. It seemed the weight of the whole team was on his shoulders. We walked in silence and I could tell he was fighting back his tears. In all of his ten years, I had never seen him so discouraged. You see, my son was the one that pitched the ball...that walked the runner...and won the game...for the other team.

We rode home in silence. He was unwilling or unable to talk about it. I searched franticly for something, anything, that I could say that would make him feel better. I had nothing. My heart broke for him. I thought about how easy it had been just to kiss away his boo boos when he was little. He is growing up and I knew instinctively that this was something he was just going to have to come to terms with on his own.... A life lesson.

He took his bath, and went to bed in silence. I went in, prayed with him, and kissed him goodnight. Oh how I wanted to tell him that it was just one game, that everyone has nights like that...but I prayed and left it in more capable hands than mine. I let him sleep in this morning, and I drove him to school. And I'd love to tell you that he was back to his sunshiny, confident, self this morning, but the truth is I could tell it was still weighing on him.

I prayed for him on my way back home. All of a sudden, it was like God dropped a song into my mouth. An old familiar song...and I began to sing, "How sweet to hold a new born baby, and feel the pride and joy he gives; But greater still the calm assurance: This child can face on certain days because He lives!"

Because He lives.... My boy is gonna be just fine!

The Question

Yesterday, for the first time ever, Rocket received a B on his report card. This morning he asked the question that I knew had been on his mind. "Are you still proud of me?" As I blinked away the tears, I assured him that I have always been, and will always be, proud of him. "I could've done better," he admitted. "I know," I said, "but that doesn't change the fact that you are my child and I have loved you since before you were born. And maybe you didn't try as hard as you could have, but that doesn't change who you are. And who you are is really great!" "Thanks Mom, I'll get my A back." "I know you will Son, but even if you didn't, these facts will never change." And with that, I got a smile, and a hug. The bus arrived and he was off to school.

There it is. This is the question. Here is what we want to know. We want to know if God is proud of us and just how long His love for us will endure. Does God really love us forever? Not just on Sunday when our shoes are shined and our hair is fixed. We want to know, how does God feel about me when I mess up, when I haven't done my best? Not when I'm peppy and positive and making all A's. Not then. I know how

He feels about me then. Even I like me then. I want to know how He feels about me when I snap at anything that moves, when my thoughts are gutter-level, when my tongue is sharp enough to slice a rock. How does He feel about me then? Did I drift too far? Wait too long? Slip too much? That's what we really want to know.

God answered our question before we could ask it. So we'd see His answer, He lit the sky with a star. So we'd hear it, He filled the night with a choir; and so we'd believe it, He did what no man had ever dreamed. He became flesh and dwelt among us. He placed His arm around the shoulder of humanity and said, "You're something special!" He saw us before we were born, and He loves what He sees. Overcome by pride, the Star-Maker turns to us, one by one, and says, "You are My child. I love you dearly. And nothing will ever change that fact."

Remember the Duck!

I once read a story about a little boy who was out shooting rocks with a slingshot. He accidentally hit his Grandmother's pet duck and killed it. He then panicked and hid the bird in the woodpile, only to look up and see his sister watching. After lunch that day, Grandma asked the girl to help with the dishes. She told her Grandmother that her brother had volunteered to do them. Before he could object, she leaned over and whispered, "Remember the duck!" So, the boy did the dishes. What choice did he have? For the next several weeks he was at the sink often. Sometimes for his duty, sometimes for his sin. "Remember the duck," his sister would whisper when he objected.

One day, he was so tired of doing the dishes, he decided any punishment would be better, so he confessed to killing the duck. "I know, Honey," his Grandmother said, giving him a hug. "I saw the whole thing from the kitchen window. Because I love you, I forgave you. I wondered how long you would let your sister make a slave out of you."

He had been pardoned, but he thought he was guilty. Why? He had listened to the words of his accuser. You have been accused as well. Every moment of your life, your accuser is filing charges against you. This expert witness has no higher goal than to take you to court and press charges. As he speaks, you hang your head. You have no defense. His charges are accurate. "I plead guilty, your honor," you mumble. "The sentence?" Satan asks. "The wages of sin is death," explains the Judge, "but in this case the death has already occurred. For this one died with Christ." Satan is suddenly silent. And you are suddenly jubilant! You realize that Satan cannot accuse you. No one can accuse you! No more dirty dishwater. No more penance. No more nagging sisters. You have stood before the Judge and heard Him declare, "Not guilty!"

I've Been Here Before

"Ugh! This is just too hard!" The frustration in my son's voice had gotten my attention. He had downloaded a new game onto my phone, and was finding it somewhat challenging. Now I know my son, and I know he has a confidence level that most would envy. He just knows "*All things are possible with God (Mark 10:27)*" so success must be imminent. So I watched and listened over the next few days when he played this new game. I'm not a gamer, but the way I understand it, until you reach a certain level, if you lose, you have to start back at the first level. By the second day, I remarked how good he was doing on the lower levels. (These had been the levels that had brought about the frustration the day before.) He smiled and said, "Yeah, I've been here before, and I know where the traps are, so I stay out of them, and I've been able to beat my high score every time I have to repeat them."

Over the next few days I noticed that he began to reach some of the higher levels, and was no longer having to start all over. I couldn't help but smile as I watched his confidence grow with each new level. He explained that with each new level, his character became bigger and stronger. Then, last night, I heard him yell, "Yes!" I went back to his room to enquire. With a huge smile on his face, he said, "I beat my high score!" "Of what level?" I asked. "Of the game!" Wow! He had managed to get through the entire game. Not once, not twice, but three times! And he had almost doubled his original score!

When I got up this morning, I found myself in an all too familiar place. A place where the enemy had defeated me (I'm sad to say) more than once. But instantly, I remembered the words of my son. "I've been here before, and I know where the traps are, so I stay out of them." Woohoo! Victory! You see, I know that with each new level our character becomes bigger and stronger too. And I could almost hear the devil and all his demons groan, as I exclaimed out loud, "I just beat my high score!"

A Perfect Love Story

Oh, how he loved her. She was second only to God in his life. She was the beautiful love of his life, and he cherished her. They had a relationship that most people would envy. It was a beautiful love story.

Then one day, she was gone. Gone to be present with the Lord. Oh how I grieved. I couldn't even imagine how he must have felt. I knew he was strong in his faith, but this was a devastating blow. And he worshiped...

She was single, married only to Jesus, her Lord and Savior...and her love for Him was obvious. She found herself at a restaurant, engrossed in his book. She knew his circumstance, how he had just lost his beautiful wife of 33 years. But she was drawn to him through this book. So she prayed and asked God if they could just be friends. What she didn't know was that God had something better in store for her, something more than she could dream or imagine.

I titled this piece "A Perfect Love Story," and by now you've probably guessed this is a 'boy meets girl' story...and now they are joined together by God, in covenant marriage. But, when I wrote the words, "A

Perfect Love Story," I wasn't referring to the love they share with each other. I was referring to God's love for him. And God's love for her. You see, God didn't leave this man bloody and wounded, and He didn't leave this woman with a yearning desire to have a husband. No, He loved them too much for that! He loved them with a perfect love…the same love He has for you…and me. Their story is truly a testament of God's love, goodness, and mercy. That, my friends, is "A Perfect Love Story."

Opposite Day

The devil is a liar...and the truth is not in him.

One afternoon, I told Rocket to get up and let the dog out. He smiled at me, teasingly, and said, "It's Opposite Day!" To which I replied, "Okay, 'don't' mind me, or I 'won't' spank you." He smiled at me again, and said, "It's 'not' okay!"

Now, I realize that "Opposite Day" is just a silly child's game, but it got me to thinking. What if God's people stepped right through 'believing' the devil is a liar into 'knowing' (I mean REALLY KNOWING) the devil is a liar? What if we REALLY knew that everything he whispered in our ear was opposite of the truth?

It would go something like this:
Devil: You're worthless.
Us: WOW! I am valuable!
Devil: You're broke, and you're always gonna be broke.
Us: Woohoo! I'm rich, and I'm always gonna be rich!
Devil: You will never amount to anything.
Us: My future is so bright, I need to wear shades!

Well, you get the picture. So, the next time the devil comes around, whispering in your ear, remember, with him it's always "Opposite Day!"

Consider the Promise

"And not being weak in faith, he did not consider his own body, already dead (since he was about a hundred years old), and the deadness of Sarah's womb. He did not waver at the promise of God through unbelief, but was strengthened in faith, giving glory to God, and being fully convinced that what He had promised He was also able to perform." (Romans 4:19-21)

Abraham didn't consider the problem, he considered the promise. He didn't worry, he trusted. Because life is sometimes difficult, and because we have fears about the uncertainty of the future, we worry. At times, we may find ourselves fretting over the countless details of everyday life. We may worry about our relationships, our finances, our health, or any number of potential problems, some large and some small.

If you think you're just a "worrier" by nature, it's probably time to rethink the way you think! Perhaps you've formed the unfortunate habit of focusing on the negative aspects of life, considering the problems instead of considering (and focusing on) the promises of God. If so, take your worries to God...and leave them there. When you do, you'll learn to worry less, and trust God more. And that's as it should be because God is trustworthy, you are protected, and your future is intensely bright.

When my faith begins to wane, help me, Lord, to trust You more. Then, with Your Holy Word on my lips and with the love of Your Son in my heart, let me live courageously, faithfully, prayerfully, and thankfully today and everyday. Amen.

The Buzzards Are Singing

One indication that it's not going to be your 'best' day is when the bird singing outside your bedroom window is a buzzard. Let's face it, there are times when we are weakened by our circumstances. There are times when it seems to be "Us vs. Life," and Life is up by three points with less than two minutes to go in the last quarter. These are the times when a 'self help' book just won't cut it. After all, no earthly author has all the answers, no matter what it says on the dust jacket of their book.

But, I have good news! God has spoken to the circumstances of our lives...when the buzzards are singing, circling, or otherwise. He doesn't send us to voice mail when we cry out to Him in pain, confusion, or grief. By the inspiration of the Holy Spirit, He instructed forty-some writers to express His concern and His promises of deliverance in the book of all books, the Bible. And when you love this Book, it'll love you back! Even when it seems our world is crumbling, and we are certain the sky is falling, if we let God take control, testing times become building times. We will not only learn to cope, we will find purpose in the pain, and more...

Risking Everything

I've been a little concerned about our dog since Rocket got his new kitten. After all she is having to share her house, her kid, and her attention with this new little fur ball. No one gets onto the cat for eating her food, but she gets scolded for eating his. He's allowed on the furniture (like we could keep him off of it), she's not, and she has three years seniority on this little pest! And if all that's not bad enough, everybody that comes in the house seems to fall in love with him!

This afternoon, when I turned on the vacuum, I did what I always do. Because it terrifies her, I put her out. It doesn't seem to bother the kitten. But when I turned it on, Noel began jumping on the door trying to get back in. She continued to jump, bark, and hit the door, until I stopped and let her in. She ran in grabbed the kitten up, and ran into my room. My first thought was, "Oh no! Seeing that the kitten was braver than she is has pushed her over the edge, and she's gonna kill him!"

I ran into the bedroom just in time to see her put him on the bed. The same bed that she herself has never been allowed to get on. She was trying to protect him from the very thing that scares her the most! The rest of the time that I vacuumed she stayed right beside the bed, careful to position herself between the kitten and the "monster."

I couldn't help but laugh, but I also couldn't help but wonder... In the same circumstance, would I have done the same thing? Risking everything for the very thing that had moved in and taken so much away from her? Instinctively, doing what was right...without any thought for herself. I hope I would have.

Keeping Christmas

It is a good thing to observe Christmas Day. It helps one to feel the supremacy of the common life over the individual life. It reminds a man to set his own little watch by the great clock of humanity, thus placing others' needs before his own...but there is a better thing than the observance of Christmas Day, and that is, keeping Christmas.

Are you willing to forget what you have done for other people, and to remember what other people have done for you; to ignore what you are owed, and to think about what you owe; to put your rights in the background, and your duties in the middle distance, and your chances to do a little more than your duty in the foreground; to see that your fellow men are just as real as you are, and try to look behind their faces to their hearts, to close your book of complaints, and look around you for a place where you can sow a few seeds of happiness...are you willing to do these things even for a day? Then you can keep Christmas.

Are you willing to stoop down and consider the needs and the desires of little children; to remember the weakness and loneliness of people who are growing old; to stop asking how much your friends love you, and ask yourself whether you love them enough; to bear in mind the things that other people have to bear on their hearts; to try to understand what those who live in the same house with you really want, without waiting for them to tell you; to trim your lamp so that it will give more light and less smoke, and to carry it in front so that your shadow will fall behind you; to make a grave for your ugly thoughts, and a garden for your kindly feelings, with the gate open. Are you willing to do these things even for a day? Then you can keep Christmas...not just one day a year, but every day of the year!

Trusting

Days like this used to really upset our dog, Noel. You see, one of her favorite things to do, is to go to the bus stop with us in the mornings. On days that Rocket didn't go to school, she would run through the house, almost panicked, trying to alert us that we needed to get out there. (She didn't do this on weekends, because somehow she knows the difference.) No amount of comforting would do. She just knew we were getting it all wrong, and eventually she would get so upset, she'd get behind the couch and refuse to come out for hours! But over the years, she's learned to trust me. She knows now, that if I don't get up with the alarm and wake Rocket up, it's just because something's changed, and she seems to trust that I have it all under control. So this morning, she came into my room like she always does, I didn't get up, so she went back to bed. It was almost as if she was saying, "Okay, I know things aren't going the way I had planned, but I trust you know what you're doing."

I couldn't help but laugh, because it seems my dog and I have so much in common. I used to be the same way with God. When things seemed to be going all wrong, I felt it was my job to alert Him. And if I didn't see Him changing the situation, panic would set in.

And then came the hours (sometimes days) of sulking, because "God just wasn't listening to me." But as time went by, as my relationship with Him grew, I discovered I could trust Him, that He knows what He's doing, and He always wants and does the best for me. I was then able to maintain my peace, whether things seemed on track or off.

Even as I write this, Noel is laying at my feet, sleeping peacefully, and a song continues to run through my mind... "Tis so sweet to trust in Jesus... Just to take Him at His Word..."

Someone To Walk With

Naomi had probably packed sandwiches and Capri sun pouches for Ruth and Orpah's journey back to their homeland. Orpah took her sack lunch with her. (Clearly she knew all she would get on the airplane was a small pack of peanuts and one-third of a can of orange juice.) Ruth turned down the lunch. The Bible records the beautiful scene in Ruth 1:16-18. It's more than a convenient scripture passage for a wedding ceremony. It was a stellar act of commitment to someone who faced more than her share of trouble. Ruth traded the smooth jet flight to Moab for the rugged journey to Judah. She put her arm around her grieving mother-in-law and said, "I'm with you."

God often uses ordinary people for extraordinary assignments. Ruth knew Naomi needed a friend. She traded the niceties of home for the uncertainties of the journey back to Judah and the life to follow. When they reached their destination, they were the talk of the town (probably because they were such a sorry sight). They had traveled hundreds of miles. Their mascara was smeared. They hadn't had their nails done in weeks. "Hello Naomi," her old friends greeted. "Do not call me Naomi!" the weary traveler replied in Ruth 1:20. "Call me Mara, because the Almighty has made my life very bitter." (NIV)

Certainly, the times were rough. She had endured about as much as any wife and mother could! But she had forgotten God's goodness in providing 'that' friend. He had injected Heaven's compassion into the veins of a Moabite woman named Ruth, and it took! God's ambassador had been with Naomi every step of the way.

We've been there, haven't we? So caught up in our grief, we don't realize that God has provided someone to walk with us during desolate times. God wouldn't fail us. His ambassadors have been appointed to our "foreign countries." God uses good relationships to help us through bad times. Danny Thomas once said, "Success has nothing to do with what you gain in life or accomplish for yourself. It's what you do for others."

Hope

When we say a situation or a person is hopeless, we are calling God a liar and slamming the door in His face. The hope that the world offers is fleeting and imperfect. However, the hope that God offers is unchanging, unshakable, and unending. It is no wonder, then, that when we seek security from worldly sources, our hopes are often dashed and our stresses are often increased. Thankfully, God has no such record of failure! Where will you place your hopes today? Will you seek solace exclusively from fallible human beings, or will you place your hopes, first and foremost, in the trusting hands of your Creator? The decision is yours...and mine, and we must live with the results of the choice we make. For believers, hope begins with God. Period. So today, as you embark upon the next stage of your life's journey, consider the words of the Psalmist: "*You are my hope; O Lord God, You are my confidence*" (Psalms 71:5 NAS). Then place your trust in the One who cannot be shaken.

Grace

Grace is the empowering presence of God mirrored in your life, enabling you to be what God has called you to be, and to do what God has called you to do.

When the enemy tries to convince you that it's not yours, that you cannot have it, show him your receipt (Bible) where it is stamped: PAID IN FULL! (Romans 8:1-2)

Receive what is now rightfully yours. Oh, and on your way out, tell the devil that you are no longer his concern!

Excuse Me, Are You Jesus?

I heard a song this morning that told the story of a man rushing to catch a flight home. On his way through the airport, he accidentally knocks over an apple stand, spilling the fruit all over the floor. He turns to see a young woman on her knees trying to recover the apples that are now scattered all over the place. He's tempted to just keep going, because he knows he will miss his flight if he stops to help. But then he realizes the young woman is blind. So he does what's right. He gets on his hands and knees and helps her pick up the apples. He puts them back like they were...and he places some money in her hand for the bruised and broken ones. She hugs him, and asks, "Excuse me, are you Jesus? Is that why you are so kind?"

So now as I sit here, as the tears stream down my face, I pray, "Oh Lord, please let me live my life in such a way that somebody will mistake me for You."

Renewing the Mind

When I began to talk to the Lord about our words, He spoke to me about our thoughts. Then I began to ask Him about feelings, and He spoke to me about "renewing the mind." I'd love to say that then this light bulb came on and I understood all that He was trying to show me, but in reality it took several days of me seeking Him to begin to scratch the surface of what He was trying to tell me.

I remembered a time when I was a new believer. I watched as someone got "set free," only to watch them fall back into old habits a few weeks later. When I had questions about this, I was taken to John 8:36. "*Therefore if the Son makes you free, you shall be free indeed.*" Then I was told, that because it says, "if," clearly the Son had not set him free, or he would not have fallen back into his old habits. Even as a new believer, that just never set right with me. I didn't know much then, but what I did know was this: Jesus is no respecter of persons (what He'll do for one, He'll do for all). Any time anyone said, "Lord, if You are willing," He was. He had come to set the captives free.

I guess at some point I had quit dwelling on it, yet here it was again, coming to the surface of my mind after all these years. I also remembered a time that Gary's aunt was healed of a breathing problem. I saw her walk into the church with oxygen on, and walk out without it! Then the same thing.. a few short weeks later...she was right back on it. Did she really get healed? Absolutely!

What she, and the other fellow didn't do was continue to renew their minds, thereby changing their mindsets. In effect they were pouring "new wine into old wine skins," and they were leaking! Everything starts with our thoughts–words, feelings, and actions. We must learn to take every thought captive, hold it up to the light of God's Word, and if it doesn't line up, pitch it out! We must renew our mindset with the washing of God's word. When we do this we put His "new wine" into new wineskins, and we are able to get on board with what He says about any given situation we face.

A friend of mine once explained it like this: You can take someone with a "poor mindset" and give them a million dollars, but before you know it they'll be broke again. Why? Because nothing changed on the inside. They still saw themselves as poor. In the same way, you can take all the money away from someone who sees himself as rich, and he will find a way to gain it all back. Mindset! When we renew our minds by the washing of the Word, we need only believe, and we are moved by what we see in the light of the lamp stand that is fueled by the oil of the Holy Spirit, not by our natural light.

Help From God

While at work, a woman received a phone call that her daughter was very sick with a fever. She left work and stopped at the pharmacy to get some medication for her daughter. She returned to her car only to find that she had locked her keys inside and was now unable to drive home. She didn't know what to do and she started to panic. She called the babysitter to check on her daughter and to inform her of the situation. The babysitter suggested that she find a coat hanger and see if that would open the door. She looked around and found an old rusty coat hanger on the ground, but had no idea how to use it to open the door. So she bowed her head and asked God to send her some help. Within five minutes, a motorcycle roared and pulled up beside her car. A rough, dirty-looking biker got off and saw her situation. He asked if he could help her. The woman thought to herself, "Really God, this is the help You sent me?" She finally said yes, explaining that she was in a hurry to get home to her daughter. In less than one minute the car was opened. She hugged the man and through her tears she said, "Thank you so much! You are such a nice man." The man replied, "No I'm not, Lady. I just got out of prison for car theft." The woman hugged him again and with sobbing tears cried out to God, "You even sent me a professional!"

Now that's the God I serve!

Reading Labels

I am a label reader. I like to know what the contents are before I commit to buy or consume any given product. I read cans, boxes, mixes, etc. Man-made labels on man-made products can be a great thing. They let us compare ingredients, fat content, carbs, etc., so that we are able to make informed decisions. But when we began to put man-made labels on God-made things, such as people, we take a wrong turn.

All too many times we see people and immediately begin to "size them up." In effect we are affixing a tag or a sticker on them, indicating their contents, the way we perceive them: too thin, too fat, too pretty, not pretty enough, not smart enough, not friendly, too this or not enough that.

God has placed His label on all people. If only we take the time to read them, we will see that His labels on people read, "Precious! Worth dying for!" And when we read His labels, then, and only then, are we able to make informed decisions about the people we encounter.

A Witness, Not a Judge

An individual Christian may see fit or feel led to give up all sorts of things. However, the moment we start looking down our noses at other people who do them, we have taken a wrong turn. Don't judge other people more harshly than you want God to judge you. All too often, Christians think they are prosecuting attorneys or judges, when in reality, God has called all of us to be witnesses.

What's Your Motivation?

For the last two nights Rocket has prayed for one of his friends to be healed. His friend cut his finger and has been unable to play baseball. I couldn't help but notice that every time he prays for him, he's quick to point out to God that his motives are pure with no hidden agenda. He says, "Not just so he can help us win ball games, but because he needs it."

It takes me back to two summers ago. We were nearing the end of June, and because it hadn't rained in weeks, we were under a burn ban. Now, like most boys, my son loves to shoot fireworks, and the 4th of July is one of his favorite times of the year. He knew that if we didn't get some rain he wouldn't be able to shoot the fireworks that we had bought. So, my then seven year old son prayed faithfully every night that it would rain. As the 4th got closer, with no rain in sight, he expressed how frustrated he was that he had been praying and still it hadn't rained. So I asked him what his motivation was. He asked me what I meant. So I asked him if he was praying for rain because we needed it so badly, or just so he could do what he wanted to do. He didn't answer me, but I could tell he was thinking about it. On July 2nd, it still hadn't rained and he went to play with a couple of his friends around noon. The other boys' mom called me and told me that she had overheard the boys talking. She said her boys were complaining about the firework situation and Rocket told them about the conversation we had had. She said afterwards they went out back and began to pray for rain. She said Rocket prayed, "Even if we don't get to shoot our fireworks, please let it rain because we need it."

Now I know this not a "parting of the red sea" kind of story, but let me tell you that at 2:15pm, on July 2, 2011, those same three boys were running, jumping, laughing, and playing...in the rain! It wasn't enough to lift the burn ban, but it did provide a nice drink to this dry, parched area that needed it so badly. The 4th came and went and his fireworks remained on the shelf unopened. Later I asked him if he was still upset about it. He said, "Nah, I'm good." "Really, what changed?" I asked. He shrugged his shoulders and said, "I don't know. I guess it just felt good to pray for the right thing, for the right reason."

Kids Today

If I said, "Kids today _____," there would be plenty of people that could and would finish that sentence. Sadly, most of us would finish it with something negative. I know, because I hear it all the time (and I've been guilty of it myself). Things like, "Kids today...don't even know what work is...have no moral fiber...have very little social skills," and the list goes on and on. Nevertheless, I have to say, I watched some of those "kids today" last night. I watched as they knelt down with their coaches, caps removed, heads bowed, eyes closed in reverence and respect as they prayed. Now our coach prays with them before every game, but last night I really watched how the boys respond to it. God has a way of speaking right to the heart of a child and I see His blessing and His favor on these young boys. Boys that will soon be growing into young men. After all, this is the next generation. I'm not worried. I'm not concerned. So let me be the first to finish that sentence: Kids today are awesome! They have a desire to learn and grow, and to fulfill God's plan and purpose for their lives. And I personally think, if we take the time to really watch them, we can probably learn a lot from them!

Free Easter Baskets

Yesterday, while driving through Hot Springs, we saw a group of people amid Easter baskets lined up on the ground. They held signs that read, "FREE EASTER BASKETS!" Of course Rocket wanted to stop and get one. Gary made the statement, "You know they're going to be asking for donations." Truthfully, I thought he was probably right, but we stopped anyway. As Rocket and I got out and approached the baskets, we were warmly welcomed by a friendly young man. He asked Rocket if he wanted a basket and told him to pick whichever one he wanted. While he went to pick a basket, the young man and I chatted. There was no mention of donations, just friendly conversation. I couldn't help but notice that inside every basket there was a Bible. Yet he never mentioned any particular church. We thanked him and left.

Inside the basket we found a Bible, a stuffed animal, and lots of candy. What we didn't find was any denominational based pamphlet, or even a church business card. There was nothing that pointed back to them. They were just placing the Word of God in the hands of children.

While I am easily amused, I am not easily impressed. But these people impressed me! They made sure it was not about them or their church. They were simply "about the Father's business."

A Dog From Heaven

A little over four years ago, my son's dog, Harley, got killed. Harley was Rocket's best friend and we were all devastated. In fact, Rocket was so tore up about it, he told me that he didn't think he would ever want another dog. However, God sometimes uses time to heal our broken hearts. So about six weeks after Harley's death, Rocket told me that he had changed his mind, and thought he would like to have another dog. I told him I thought we ought to pray about it before we did anything else. He agreed. His prayer went something like this, "God, you know we live out in the country and sometimes I get lonely. So Lord, I was thinking that I'd like to have another dog. But I don't want just any dog, I want the dog that You have for me. So I'm going to wait on You. Oh, and God, thank You." (I remember that last part clearly.)

That all took place on a Friday night. The next day, my granddaughter was over playing with him in the yard, when all of a sudden she came running through the door and exclaimed, "Meemo, Rocket found a puppy!" I figured it probably belonged to one of our neighbors so I went to see. As I rounded the corner of the house, I saw my son holding this little scraggly, mangy, bag of bones. And she smelled worse than she looked! But there he stood, holding this pitiful little pup up next to his heart and smiling like he had found a great treasure. "Look Mom! Oh look what God gave me! He gave me a puppy just like I asked for!" I said, "Oh Son, does it have to be this puppy?" I'll never forget the look of confusion and disappointment on my son's face at that moment. With his most serious tone, he asked, "How are you gonna do that?" "Do what, Son?" "Ask God for something, and then when He gives it to you, tell Him it's not good enough."

That day, we started the long process of getting her well. I simply did not have the money to take her to the vet, so I got on my computer and typed in all her symptoms, and began every home remedy we could find. Every day Rocket and I laid hands on her, and we prayed. We prayed for healing. We prayed for wisdom. Some days we just prayed for strength! One day I walked in and found her dripping with oil from head to toe. Rocket had anointed her! He said, "I wasn't sure how much to use, so just to be safe I poured the whole thing on her!" I might mention at this point, that "the whole thing" he was referring to, was a $65 bottle of olive oil, which incidentally, was sitting in the cabinet right beside a cheap bottle of olive oil.

We had tried everything, but she just wasn't getting any better. So, once more we prayed, and I called the vet. I'll never forget the conversation I had that day with the lady that answered the phone. I explained the whole situation to her, including the part where I didn't have any money. She said that because Noel (that's what he named her) was basically a "rescue" to go ahead and bring her in and they'd let me pay it out. Wow God! And so it began...she started the long journey that would lead to happy and healthy.

One day, I asked Rocket if he'd ever thanked God for Noel, and he assured me that he had. "Did you?" he asked. "Well, yes Son, I did." "Oh, I didn't know that you knew," he said. "Knew what?" I asked. "That she was worth saving." I stood there that day, broken...broken before my God and my son...knowing full well that that's what God sees when He looks at us. Even when we're at our worst, He sees something "worth saving."

It took us about two years to get Noel completely well. One day I made a remark to Rocket about how "pretty" she is now. He said, "What do you mean 'now'?" And once again I was reminded of how God sees us. Rocket had never seen what I saw the first time I laid eyes on this pup that God had used to teach me so much. All he had ever seen was the beautiful gift that God had given him.

Now, as you've probably guessed, Noel has turned out to be the best dog we've ever had. And it's not uncommon for people to mention how impressed they are that she is so good-natured, well behaved, and obedient. The other day, I overheard one of Rocket's friends talking about how "good" she is. He asked, "Where did you get her anyway?" I smiled as I heard my son give the answer that I knew he would give: "God gave her to me."

True Love

As I think of Valentine's Day, I consider the fact that while some look forward to this day, others really dread it. For some, it means goose bumps and warm fuzzies, for others it's just one more reminder of what they don't have and an awareness of being alone. But let me encourage all of you today, to take this day and celebrate Love...Real Love...God's Love. "*For God so loved the world that He sent His only begotten Son, that whosoever believes in Him will not perish, but have everlasting life*" (John 3:16). Now that's reason for celebration! God Loves you! And me!

A Call to Pray

When my alarm went off this morning, I discovered that Rocket was already up. "What are you doing?" I asked. "Praying," he answered. I asked if anything was bothering him. His answer was, "No." I said, "So nothing's wrong, and you just got up to pray?" He said, "Yep, I heard Jesus calling my name."

It felt as if a ray of sunlight had just streamed through my living room! I stood there silently praying, "Oh Lord help me to always hear Your voice, Your call to pray, not just because it makes me a better person, but because You enjoy spending time with me."

Fear Came Knocking On My Little Boy's Heart

My son has a confidence that most adults (including me) would envy. He knows who he is, and just believes success is imminent. Usually.

He came to me last night and told me that he didn't want to sing in the church Christmas program. He had been asked to do a duet with another boy, and said he "didn't think he could do it!" I knew 'fear' had come knocking at his heart, so I prayed...

Nevertheless, I spoke to the director of the program, and explained that he just really didn't want to do it. While she said it was "fine," she seemed genuinely surprised. She said she had bought one boy gift and one girl gift for the children who had put out the best effort. She confided in me that she had bought the boy gift for Rocket. I knew right then the enemy had used fear to steal a gift that was meant for my son.

When we got home I could tell it was still weighing heavy on his mind. So I asked, "Want to talk about it?" All his doubts and fears came rushing out like a flood. He said, "I know I can't do it, I'm just not good enough! I'm afraid I'll mess it up!" I talked to my son for quite awhile. I explained that God gives us strength when we need it. There is no promise of grace before we need it. God doesn't say He will strengthen our arms for the battle when there is no battle. When conflict is approaching, we are given necessary strength. He doesn't open the gates for us nor roll away the stones until we come to them. He did not divide the waters of the Jordan while the people were still in their camps, nor even when they began to march toward the river. The wild stream continued to flow even as the feet of the priests dipped in the water. This is the continual law of God's divine help in time of need. It is not given in advance, but as we come to the need, He's already there ready to meet it. This is where we truly learn that we can believe in the dark what we heard Him say in the light.

Rocket said, "I almost forgot." "Forgot what?" I asked. "That He said He was always with me." We went back to the church last night to let the director know that he had changed his mind. His faith was strengthened, knowing that when he steps up to sing he won't be alone.

As for fear...well, fear just had to leave!

Looking At the Heart

A few months ago, Rocket came home and told me about a child at school (I'll call him Bill) who the other children were making fun of. He said they were calling him names because of his weight. He told me he had decided to be his friend. I knew my son was moved with compassion. Over the next few weeks, he continued to mention Bill from time to time.

Yesterday, however, he came home chattering on and on about him. He began to tell me how interesting Bill is and how well he can draw, on and on...

I knew it had happened. What started out as a seed of compassion had now grown into a tree of friendship and was producing fruit! You see, when my son looks at Bill now, he no longer sees "the fat kid" as the others called him. He just sees his friend. He now sees Bill like God sees him.

For the Lord does not see as man sees; for man looks at the outward appearance, but the Lord looks at the heart (1Samuel 16:7b).

Proof of God's Love

A couple of weeks ago, while at a football game, I noticed a woman who was struggling to fix a flat tire. As I approached her to see how I could help, I couldn't help but notice all the pentagram jewelry she was wearing. She even had a pentagram tattooed on her neck. Instantly I felt a little intimidated. What I had seen as an opportunity to "minister" had somehow fallen short and silent. I even wondered if I would have stopped if I had been able to see her from a distance. Then I heard God say, "I love her, do you?" I had Gary get our jack and we helped her fix her flat. As she drove off, she called out to me, "You know, the world's a better place because you're in it!" I stood there silently praying, "Oh God let that be true!" I was reminded of a line in one of my favorite songs, "Let my life be the proof of Your love, let my love look like You and what You're made of."

Going Through to the Other Side

As I read Exodus 3:6-10, I can't help but notice that God said, "*I have seen the way the Egyptians are oppressing them.*" God has an eye on the events of our lives. He not only saw His people's problems, but He was going to do something about them. Moses, the faithful fugitive, got the message; God wants me to quit tending *sheep* and start tending *people*. Thousands of them! As nervous as a cockroach at a bug-exterminator convention, Moses replied, "*Who am I that I should go to Pharaoh and bring the Israelites out of Egypt?*" (Exodus 3:11, NIV) In other words, "Hold the phone! Can't we talk about this first, Lord?" We often argue with God about our adversities, saying, "Why me Lord?" or "Can't we talk about this first Lord?"

But the truth is, it's those times of tests and trials that build us and make us stronger. After all, greatness isn't determined by what it takes to get someone going. Greatness is determined by what it takes to stop them! "Tis so sweet to trust in Jesus, just to take Him at His Word..."

Man's Best "Friend"

My husband, Gary and our dog Noel just don't get along very well. The problem is not her personality. A sweeter mutt you will not find. She sees everyone as a friend and every day as a holiday. He has no problem with her attitude, the problem is with her habits – eating scraps out of the trash, refusing to go outside if it's hot or raining, even if it's just long enough to do her business. Once while I was in the hospital, he let her in after she had been out for a while, she went into the living room and proceeded to urinate in the floor. Shameful! She rolls in the grass, chews on herself (loudly), and even though we make sure she always has fresh water, she prefers to quench her thirst in the toilet. Now what kind of behavior is that? Dog behavior, you'd reply, and you'd be right.

Noel's problem is not a Noel problem. Noel has a dog problem. It's a dog's nature to do such things. And it's her nature Gary wishes to change. We could send her to obedience school to change her behavior, that is what she does; but Gary wants to go deeper. He wants to change who she is. He would like to do a Gary–to–Noel transfusion, the deposit of a Gary seed in Noel. He would like to give her a kernel of human character. As it grew, would she not change? We would witness not just a change of habits, but a change of essence. She would have a new nature. You think this plan is crazy? Then take it up with God. The idea is His. What Gary would like to do with Noel, God does with us. He changes our nature from the inside out! God doesn't send us to obedience school to learn new habits; He literally replaces our old heart with a new one. Forget training, He gives transplants.

My Faith and My Foot

I got bit by a copperhead seventeen days ago, and have been in the hospital until today. When I arrived at the hospital, the surgeon who took my case told me that he was going to do everything that he could to save my foot. I told him that I am a praying woman, and that I had every intention of leaving the hospital with my faith and my foot intact. He patted my hand and said okay, much like you would a confused mental patient, to keep from upsetting him.

I had five surgeries in a little over two weeks, and I'm not ever going to pretend it was anything but hard. In fact, it was downright grueling. I did, however, get several chances to minister while I was there, and there are a couple that really stand out in my mind.

The first was a youth pastor's wife. She confessed that she knew about God, but wasn't sure that she knew Him personally. I prayed with her, and now she has no doubt that she is not just going through the motions, but has a relationship with Jesus Christ.

The second one was a young lady who worked in food service. She was convinced that she was and always would be trapped in depression. I had the honor of introducing her to the one that came to set the captives free. God is so good!

After my last surgery, the doctor came in to talk to me. He began to explain how, even though he had removed a large amount of skin from my foot, somehow he was still able to close it up without a skin graft. He said in twelve years this was the worst he had ever seen, but it was responding so well to the surgery and treatment that he was going to let me go home five days earlier than he had originally planned. He never used the word "miracle," but I'm pretty sure he wanted to. He did, however, say that he couldn't explain it. Ha! Ha! I'm home now...with my faith and my foot intact! To all of you who stood for me when I couldn't stand for my self, thank you. God used this experience to change the hearts and lives of many, including my own.

Ode to a Wounded Heart

My Grandmother used to say, "The proof is in the pudding." While I don't quite understand the reference to pudding, I do get the basic concept. We have all heard the saying, "Sticks and stones may break my bones, but words can never hurt me." Nothing could be farther from the truth! I guess I'm just tired of people saying, "I love you," while their actions prove this to be untrue. It always leaves me wounded, dazed, and confused. We should never make a statement of that magnitude unless we mean it, and intend to back it up with our actions. The Bible tells us in 1 Corinthians 13:4-7 what love is...and what love is not. Without these guide lines, "I love you" just becomes idle words (idle meaning "useless and barren.") We must be careful not to wound others, by casually throwing around the very words that are meant to bring healing. We should never say, "I love you," unless we are prepared, and willing to back it up with our actions.

Danger Zone

I dropped my son off at football practice. As I started to exit the field I noticed a girl standing just a few feet from the end zone. As I walked by her, I heard her say, "If they hit me with one of those balls I'm gonna be mad!" I said, "Well sweetie, you are in the danger zone, and the chances of you getting hit here are pretty good. Maybe you should move to a safer area." With her feet squared up, she said, "Nope, I'm gonna stand here; and they better not hit me!"

I couldn't help but think of all the similarities between this rebellious little girl and Christians (I'm including myself) today. The Word tells us that God always provides us a way out. However, He will not force us to take it. We stand there getting pounded with one 'ball' right after another, crying out, "Why do these things always happen to me?" We refuse to admit that our own choices brought us to, and keep us in, the 'danger zone.' After all, that would mean we would have to take responsibility, and it would make it really hard to blame others, even the ones that are throwing the balls that keep hitting us. When we choose to remain in the 'danger zone' we become frustrated, angry, depressed, and bitter.

There is a 'safe zone.' There is another way. But God will not drag us from the 'danger zone' into the 'safe zone.' He does, however, continually call out to us, in hopes that we will trust Him, and follow Him to the place that He has prepared for us. A place where we are safe and secure in the shelter of His arms.

A Mother's Words of Wisdom

"I know something the prince never knew...that all too soon the clock will strike midnight and she'll be gone." (from *Cinderella* by Steven Curtis Chapman)

Today I'm going to tell you something I've never told another soul. I keep a list. Anyone who knows me knows that I'm not a list maker. No, I'm more of a "fly by the seat of your pants" kind of girl. I don't even make grocery lists. (It drives Gary crazy!) But I do keep one list...there, I'm out of the closet! I call this my growing birthday list. Every year on my children's birthdays, I add at least one thing, sometimes more. I list one area they have grown in. I guess it's a "growth chart" really. Anyway, I list this one (or more) thing(s), and then I pray over my child and ask God to seal this 'growth' into their hearts.

As the years go swiftly by, I've watched as my role has completely changed in the lives of my grown children. My new role requires that I practice the art of verbal restraint. There are times when my daughters simply can't receive instruction from me. What they really need is for me to listen and empathize. This requires discipline. Lots and lots of discipline...and sometimes my heart cries out for another opportunity to offer words of wisdom. From start till now, the journey has benefited me though. Today is my oldest daughter's birthday. She is and has been grown for some time now. As I walk through this period of life with Brandee, I'm reminded of the many times God must feel the same frustration with me. He waits patiently for me to seek Him. He possesses all the wisdom (I'm not saying that I do) and knowledge I could ever need. He's willing to guide me and happy to counsel me. Yet, sometimes I'm slow to ask. Dare I expect more from my own children? Moving out of the way of God's work in Brandee's life, I began to understand my role. My voice wasn't to remain silent. It was to be used as needed...upon request and, most importantly, as an intercessor. My job is to cover her in prayer and trust God with her future. I have complete faith that Brandee will walk in the *"promise of the eternal inheritance"* (Hebrews 8:15) that is set before her. To that end, I pray specific prayers based on God's Word. I have received another chance to offer up words of wisdom, after all, as powerful words of prayer rise daily from my heart, I am confident that God will finish the good work He started in my little girl, and as for the "list," today I added "her ability to get back up." Because it simply isn't in her to stay down. She's either up...or getting up!

Love In Action

I got to go to Rocket's football practice Friday night. It was the first chance I've had since I got out of the hospital. Now I love to go to my son's sports practices almost as much as I love to go to his games. I was thankful to be there, but, because it's very difficult to get in and out of the truck right now, I was a little disappointed that I couldn't see very well because of the distance between us. I spotted the group I normally sit with, and wished I could get up there to see a little better and maybe visit a bit. As I looked up I saw one of the moms headed toward me. Now I want you to know I have always enjoyed visiting with this woman at practices and games, but I really don't know her very well. She came up to the window and hugged me like she meant it. She made sure I didn't feel left out...And she made sure I knew she cared. She not only stayed with me through the entire practice, she got her nail-kit out of her car and proceeded to polish my fingernails (she's very talented) into a beautiful design.

I couldn't help but cry. I knew I had experienced God's love first hand...that love that is so selfless you find yourself just melting into it...that love that goes so far beyond words that they need not even be spoken. I know to this woman it may have been just conversation and nail polish, but to me it was love in action. I pray that I never miss an opportunity to let God's love flow through me and onto someone else.

In loving memory of Felicia Huff

Adaptable

Adaptable...that's a word I really like. Happy are the adaptable. It makes a lot of sense in our world. I certainly need to be more adaptable. It's not only my world that is changing, my home is too, constantly. The only sure thing about my schedule for any given day is that it will change. God has used the circumstances of my life to make me more flexible.

What a good thing it is that God created us with a built-in ability to change. The unhappy people are the ones who feel threatened by the changes going on around them. They look to traditions and institutions to give them a sense of security. Newness frightens them. They become rigid, and in their presence there is no peace.

However, there are others that haven't hardened. Their trust in Christ is so real, and the security He gives them is so strong, they cannot be threatened by change. They realize that if they themselves are going to expand and grow, they too must change. But they are not dominated by change, they are free to evaluate it, to reject it, or accept it, according to its merits. These are the meek people. "*Blessed are the meek, for they shall inherit the earth*" (Matthew 5:5).

Serve Him With Gladness

I've been thinking about that word "glad." We don't use it much anymore. It's an old fashioned word. Remember how it used to show up in our hymns and songs? We used to sing, "Oh! Say, but I'm Glad," and "Glad day!"

Somehow "glad" has gotten pushed aside by other terms like "happy" and "upbeat." Yet in my favorite translation of the Bible, the word "glad" occurs nearly 150 times. As I peruse those verses, I come away feeling we have an obligation to serve the Lord gladly. Not just to serve Him, but to serve Him gladly and do so today.

A disheartened believer is a poor recommendation for the Christian faith! There can be joy in even the most menial task. Nothing is drudgery if the Lord is in it! Wherever we are is holy ground if the Lord is there, and He is. If you want to find strength for every day, cultivate a joyful heart. If you want to rekindle a passion for your faith, cultivate a glad spirit. If you want to win someone to Christ, cultivate a winsome attitude. If you want to recover the purpose of Christian service, make up your mind to serve the Lord today with joy.

Finally, we should serve the Lord gladly today because others need it. We pass along attitudes to others, and our sadness or gladness becomes contagious. Today is the day to be a light shining in a dark world, fueled by the joy of the Lord. "*I was glad when they said to me, 'Let us go into the house of the Lord*'" (Psalms 122:1).

What Do You Want? (John 1:38)

"What do you want?" Jesus asks you.

It is such a simple question, and yet you know that how you answer that question is going to shape the rest of your days.

"I saw you following me," Jesus says. You turn to your friend as a slight blush washes across your face. Then you look back to Jesus. His compelling force is so great that you don't concern yourself with being embarrassed.

Standing there, poised between your old life and the future, you feel alive as never before. Time seems to stand still. All the colors around you are vivid; the sounds are clear and almost musical.

What do you say when Jesus asks you what you want? Do you even know what you want? As you stand there, enclosed in a holy space, even in the midst of a crowd, you examine your heart.

Are you coming to Jesus out of curiosity? Do you have some need He might meet or an intellectual question He might answer? Is there something in you that needs to be healed? Is there some brokenness, a piercing or unrelenting pain? A failure from your past you'd like Him to carry? Do you need forgiveness? Are you dying for love? Is there something you've tried to fix that escapes your skill?

Tell Him exactly what you need. He's waiting...

He's Not Mad At Me

I remember a day, about a year and a half ago, my little boy had made a really bad choice. After his dad and I talked to him about it, we disciplined him, and then we prayed with him. After a while I went looking for him only to find him laying on his bed sobbing. I started to tell him it's because we love him that we discipline him, but he assured me that wasn't why he was crying. He said, "I made Jesus sad." I was quick to tell him that Jesus was not mad at him. He said, "I'm not crying because He's mad at me, I'm crying because He's not." With a grateful heart, I laid and held my little boy as he wept because he was completely overwhelmed by God's love, mercy, and forgiveness. Wow!

Loving...Caring...Doing

Life, in a way, is like those electric bumper cars at the amusement park. We just run into each other, smile and bump, and away we go. "How are you doing?" Bump, bump. "Great, fantastic." Bump, bump. Somebody slips out and dies because there is no one to talk to. Bump, bump, bump. What a haunting picture of our broken world.

Hundreds of hurting people, pretending to "have it all together," are laughing, talking, and hiding their pain behind a superficial smile. I can't help but wonder how many times I've bumped into people, how many times I've asked how they were doing, but not in a way that made them want to tell me. How many of them slipped out into the night and died, just a little on the inside, because they had no one to talk to? I mean really talk to.

Yet even as they pretend, while they are clever and convincing, they are desperately hoping that we won't be taken in by their empty act, that we won't let them get away with it. "Don't be fooled by me. Don't be fooled by the face I wear. I wear a mask. I wear a thousand masks, masks that I am afraid to take off; and none of them are me. I give the impression that I am secure, that confidence is my name, and coolness is my game, that I am in command; and that I need no one. But please don't believe me!"

"Who am I?" you may wonder. I am someone you know very well. I am every man, woman, and child you meet. I am right in front of you. Please...Love me...

Rejoice

Standing alone in the dark solitude of the back yard, sipping a cup of coffee and looking at the distant tree-row of the woods that surround our house, I listened as the crickets sang with lusty, joyful abandon. I couldn't help looking at everything and saying as God did, "It is good." Only *my* voice had a touch of wonder in it, while *His* only had satisfaction.

So many days are spent chasing obligations in circles and nothing special seems to stand out as worth remembering. However, five such unexpected minutes alone with God, just being still and truly seeing, truly appreciating, are worth a lifetime of chasing.

Canceled Debts

There are things I find difficult to forget, significant things, like times I have wronged or hurt someone – even when forgiveness has been extended by both God and man. That kind of memory can remind God's kids of lessons learned and prevent repeat offenses. What we must not do is remain in bondage to those memories. (See 1John 1:9 and Romans 8:1.)

Here is God's attitude: "*He does not treat us as our sins deserve or repay us according to our iniquities... As far as the East is from the West, so far has he removed our transgressions from us*" (Psalm 103:10,12, NIV).

We can never change the fact that a sin has been committed, but we can...we must...forgive those who have wronged us. We must also accept forgiveness when it has been given to us. When God forgives your sin, it is gone and He will not bring it up against you.

A debt only needs to be canceled once.

God Always Has the Last Word

I was talking to a young woman this morning. I met her only a few weeks ago, but I knew almost instantly that it was a God directed encounter. She was having a HUGE struggle in her life. I watched as she trusted God even when it was really hard. This morning I got to hear how God had showed up and showed out in her situation. Most of us just want Jesus to instantly step up to calm the troubled sea that is our lives, but there are times when God is saying to just stand and see what I'm going to do in your life through this storm (Exodus 14:13).

Romans 5:3 says, *"And not only that, but we also glory in tribulations, knowing that tribulation produces perseverance; and perseverance, character; and character, hope."* It goes on to say hope doesn't fail. So, I pray that you won't fight the hand that He is holding out to lead you through whatever it is your going through today.

Be encouraged, be blessed!

Perception

Perception is a powerful thing. If we see ourselves defeated, there's a solid chance we will be. When we see ourselves victorious (which is simply seeing ourselves as God sees us), we are!

I woke up this morning thinking about something Rocket said to me when he was seven. When asked how he always managed to get a hit in baseball, he said, "I see myself hitting the ball before I ever step up on the plate." That's powerful, and I've never forgotten it.

Now I know we all fall down. I fall down. But I see myself getting back up even on the way down. And I do. Not because I'm so good, but because God is so good. And I trust Him, When He says, "I will not leave you nor forsake you."

I pray that you will see yourself and your situation the way God sees it, this day. Many blessings, my friends!

Remembering My Friend

As I sit down to write this morning, I find that it's a struggle. I find myself heartbroken. You see, I want to find words to honor my friend who passed away this week...maybe some words that would sum things up, and possibly make sense out of all this. But I cannot find them within myself.

Felicia was my friend. I miss her tremendously; and I find myself weeping bitterly for her children. As I poured out my heart like water before the Lord, I see these words of D. L. Moody: "Someday you will read in the papers that Moody is dead. Don't you believe a word of it. At that moment I shall be more alive than I am now. I was born of the flesh in 1837, I was born of the spirit in 1855. That which is born of the flesh may die. That which is born of the spirit shall live forever."

I continue to set my hopes firmly in my Savior, and hold firmly to the promise of eternal life, remembering that when we give our hearts to the Son, we belong to the Father...today, tomorrow, and for all eternity!

Pondering the Love of our Father

On the way to school this morning, I turned down the radio, put my hand on Rocket's shoulder and said, "Son, you're something special." He looked up and smiled tolerantly. "Someday some pretty girl is going to steal your heart and sweep you into the next century; but right now, you belong to me." He tilted his head, looked at me, and said, "Why are you acting so weird?" LOL! I suppose such words sound strange to an eleven year old boy. The love of a parent falls awkwardly on the ears of a child. My burst of emotion was beyond him. But that didn't keep me from speaking.

And there's no way our little minds can comprehend the love of God. But that didn't keep Him from coming. And we too, have tilted our heads. Like Rocket, we have wondered what He was doing. From the manger in Bethlehem to the cross in Jerusalem, we've pondered the love of our Father. God's grace is launched like fireworks, not to bring answers, but to bring amazement...Oh how He loves you, and me!

Redeemed

A few years ago, I received a letter from my car insurance company. I'm glad the letter wasn't sent from heaven. I didn't drop them, they dropped me. I was dropped for making too many mistakes. Wait a minute. Let me see if I get this right. I bought insurance to cover my mistakes...but then I get dropped for making mistakes. Did I miss something?

But the fact is that reckless driving has it's consequences...so does reckless living. Just as I had no defense before the insurance company, I have no defense before God. My record accuses me. My past convicts me.

Now, suppose the CEO of the insurance company chose to have mercy on me. What can he do? Can he just close his eyes and pretend I made no mistakes? Take my driving record and tear it up? No. The integrity of the company would be compromised. The CEO is faced with a dilemma. How can he be merciful and fair at the same time? Or, to put it in biblical terms, how can God punish the sin and love the sinner? Is God going to lower His standards so I can be forgiven? Is God going to look away and pretend that I never sinned? Would we want a God who altered rules and made exceptions? No. We want a God who "*does not change like shifting shadows*" (James 1:17, NIV) and who "*judges all people by the same standard*" (1 Peter 1:17, GNT). Holiness demands that sin be punished. Mercy compels that the sinner be loved. How can God do both?

Let me answer that question by returning to the insurance executive. Imagine him calling me into his office and saying these words: "Mrs. Claborn, I have found a way to deal with all your mistakes. I can't overlook them; to do so would be unjust. I can't pretend that you didn't commit them, that would be a lie. But here's what I can do. In our records we found a person with a spotless past. He has no violations, not one trespass, not even a parking ticket. He has volunteered to trade records with you. We'll take your name and put it on his record. We'll take his name and put it on yours. We will punish him for what you did. You, who did wrong, will be made right. He, who did right will be made wrong."

Sin is still sin. God is still holy. And you...well, you are redeemed!

Struggling With Change

"The Lord is my strength and my shield; my heart trusted in Him, and I am helped; therefore my heart greatly rejoices, and with my song I will praise Him." (Psalms 28:7)

I sometimes struggle with change. In fact, I almost always struggle with change. I had been asking God to let us sell my Tahoe, and help us to find a smaller car that would get good gas mileage. Ask and you shall receive! Yesterday we sold the Tahoe, and purchased a little Sunfire. When we went out to go to the bus stop this morning, I couldn't help but miss my much roomier Tahoe. Even though we had prayed for direction before making this decision, and everything seemed so right, now it seemed all wrong. Noel (our dog), who LOVES to go to the bus stop, refused to even get into our new small car. As I struggled to coax her into the back seat, I couldn't help but laugh, thinking how much my canine and I have in common. We downsized so we would be able to do the things we love without gas prices bankrupting us..things like ministry, Rocket's games and practices, going to see our grown children and grandchildren, etc. This car opens up huge opportunities for us, and don't forget, God gave me just what I asked for. Yet there I was with my dog, both of us feeling uneasy with the change. Once I convinced Noel to get into the new back seat, and she realized we were headed to the bus stop, she became her normal bubbly self again.

Lord, help me see Your goodness in this change and give me Your guidance, too, as I adjust to it. Help me to always trust You enough to trade the familiar for the unknown. Amen.

Grace and Forgiveness

To believe we are totally and eternally debt free is seldom easy. Even if we stood before the throne and heard it from the King Himself, some would still doubt, not because the grace of the King is limited, but because our faith is.

God is willing to forgive all. He wants to wipe our slate completely clean. He guides us to a pool of mercy and invites us to bathe. Some plunge in, but others just touch the surface. They leave feeling unforgiven, and as a result, find it hard to forgive others. Where the grace of God is missed, bitterness is born; but where the grace of God is embraced, forgiveness flourishes. The longer we walk in the garden, the more likely we are to smell like flowers. The more we immerse ourselves in grace, the more likely we are to give grace. Could this be the clue for coping with anger, bitterness, and an inability to receive and release forgiveness? Could it be the secret is not in demanding payment but in pondering the payment of your Savior? Perhaps the key to forgiving others is to quit focusing on what they did "to" you and start focusing on what God did "for" you. Many Blessings, my friends!

Indescribable Value

As I scroll through Facebook this morning, I find myself looking at all the old school pictures. Mostly of younger, athletic school girls. It takes me back to my own school days, but there are no pictures for me to share. Because the fact is, I wasn't pretty and I wasn't popular. There wasn't an athletic bone in my body. (And now I find it funny that God has me raising a boy whom it seems every bone in his body is athletic.) I was painfully shy, and sadly, I got my self-worth from how I saw myself and how I perceived that others saw me. In fact, I probably learned to draw because it was something I could do alone.

I once heard a story of thieves who broke into a jewelry store and didn't steal anything; they simply rearranged the price tags. The next morning, the expensive jewelry was sold as junk, and the junk jewelry was sold as expensive. I hope my point is obvious. We live in a world where someone has rearranged the price tags.

Nowhere is this switching of price tags more evident than in the area of self-worth. In our culture, people are valued for how they look, what they can do or even what they have, but rarely for who they are. In our world, you have to be beautiful by mathematical standards (and yes there is a formula for beauty–it's all about ratios), entertaining (not talented, but entertaining), and if you are not, the world has no place for you. If you can't make the Top 100 in the world on some list, you are nothing.

This pressure on self-worth has devastating consequences in the lives of our young adults. Young men commit heinous acts just to prove to someone they are a man. Young women get involved in destructive relationships because they are told they are nothing if they do not follow the culture's standards.

Every day I'm reminded of how important the gospel message is: You are loved! You didn't do anything to earn it or deserve it, but God gives it freely! It's grace! You are created in His image, paid for by His death and invited to live a new way with Him in His resurrection. You are valuable...indescribably so...and it is only the good news of Jesus that tells you that.

Paintings are valuable because the artist signs them. Imagine...please, take a few minutes to imagine...what some museum would say you were worth if you could show them the signature of God upon you. That's what the Imago Dei means: God, the greatest Artist, has signed you and me. Our self-worth is not based on what we have done, but in who made us.

We are deemed beautiful, not by some arbitrary standard of the world, but by our Maker. God has created us and loves us. That makes us...every one of us...beautiful, because we are the bearers of God's beauty.

When you know what you are worth, things change. Your life changes. What will you change about your life, as you understand the value God has given you?

The Heart of a King

Every year, I draw something for Rocket's teacher at Christmas time. It's become a tradition, so no matter how many pieces of artwork I have to do, I always allow some time in my schedule for it. This year, however, Rocket came to me with a request. He asked me to do one more. It was for a coach; but not just any coach. This guy is someone my son really looks up to. I think Rocket met him when he was in first grade and he's admired him ever since. Anyway, he came to me and asked me to do a piece of artwork for "coach." But not just any piece of artwork. No, he had something specific in mind. I was already running behind and what he wanted was going to take some time...but, he's my son, and I could see this was important to him, so I did the only thing I could do: I got to work. I finished it last night, and we got it wrapped and give-ready.

This morning, he came to me, wallet in hand. He wanted to know "how much he owed me." I wanted to laugh, but I could see that he was serious. So I said, "Son, you don't owe me anything. You're my son and everything I have is yours. I was glad to do it for you!" His serious expression never changed and I could tell he was carefully choosing his words. "How would that be from me?" "What do you mean?" I asked. "If I don't pay for it, how is that from me? I don't want to give him something that didn't cost me anything."

My thoughts immediately went to 2Samuel 24. King David had gotten himself into a bit of a pickle and he wanted to build an alter and offer God a sacrifice. He approaches a fellow named Araunah and asks to buy his threshing room floor. Araunah tells King David that he can have it. In fact, he goes on to say, *"Let my lord the king take and offer up whatever seems good to him. Look, here are oxen for burnt sacrifice, and threshing implements and the yokes of the oxen for wood. All these, O king, Araunah has given to the king."* (v. 22) In other words, "Just take whatever you want. You don't owe me anything. I freely give it to you!" But David responds by saying that he will not give God something that cost him nothing.

I must have gotten a little too quiet for a little too long because Rocket asked if I was okay. I told him I couldn't be better. I set a price...and he gladly paid it... All the while I was silently thanking God for speaking to me once more through this little boy. I prayed that God would protect this wonderful heart He has placed within my son...after all, he has the heart of a king.